D0443570

The Wright Brothers Fly

The
Wright Brothers
Fly

By Robyn O'Sullivan

NATIONAL GEOGRAPHIC

WASHINGTON, D.C.

Founded in 1888, the National Geographic Society is one of the largest nonprofit scientific and educational organizations in the world. It reaches more than 285 million people worldwide each month through its official journal, NATIONAL GEOGRAPHIC, and its four other magazines; the National Geographic Channel; television documentaries; radio programs; films; books; videos and DVDs; maps; and interactive media. National Geographic has funded more than 8,000 scientific research projects and supports an education program combating geographic illiteracy.

For more information, please call
1-800-NGS-LINE (647-5463) or write to the following address:

National Geographic Society
1145 17th Street N.W.
Washington, D.C. 20036-4688
U.S.A.

Visit us online at www.nationalgeographic.com/books

For information about special discounts for bulk purchases, please contact
National Geographic Books Special Sales at ngspecsales@ngs.org

For rights or permissions inquiries, please contact National Geographic
Books Subisidiary Rights: ngbookrights@ngs.org

Copyright © 2007 National Geographic Society

Text revised from *The Wright Brothers* in the National Geographic Windows on Literacy program from National Geographic School Publishing, © 2004 National Geographic Society

Published by National Geographic Society. Washington, D.C. 20036

Design by Project Design Company
Photo Editor: Annette Kiesow
Project Editor: Anita Schwartz

Printed in the United States

Library of Congress Cataloging-in-Publication Data

O'Sullivan, Robyn.
 The Wright brothers fly / by Robyn O'Sullivan.
    p. cm. -- (National Geographic history chapters)
 ISBN 978-1-4263-0188-9 (library)
1. Wright, Orville, 1871-1948--Juvenile literature. 2. Wright, Wilbur, 1867-1912--Juvenile literature. 3. Wright Flyer (Airplane) 4. Aeronautics--United States--History--Juvenile literature. I. Title.
 TL540.W7O88 2007
 629.130092'273--dc22
 [B]

                2007007895

Photo Credits

Front Cover: © Getty Images; Spine, Endpaper: © Jim Sugar/CORBIS; 2-3, 6, 8-9, 9 (inset), 10, 13, 14, 15, 19, 26, 29 (inset), 32, 34, 35: © Library of Congress; 10 (inset): © Australian Picture Library/CORBIS; 12, 22, 24: © Courtesy of Special Collections and Archives, Wright State University; 16: © CORBIS; 18: © Shutterstock; 20-21: © Photolibrary.com; 23: © The Granger Collection, NY; 28-29: © Bettmann/CORBIS; 30-31: © Illustration by Jack McMaster from First To Fly, a Madison Press Book

Endsheets: A close-up of the wings of the Wright Flyer, on display at the Smithsonian in Washington, D.C.

Contents

Katharine Wright, wearing a leather jacket, cap, and goggles, sits with her brother Orville aboard the Wright Model HS airplane.

The Age of Flight

Something amazing happened on the sandy beach at Kitty Hawk, North Carolina, on December 17, 1903. Two brothers were on the beach that morning. They had a flying machine they had built themselves. Orville Wright took off in the machine. He flew a distance of 120 feet (37 meters) in the air before landing again.

It was the world's first successful powered airplane flight. The Wright brothers' airplane, *Flyer 1*, was powered by an engine. The pilot lay on the bottom wing next to the engine. He steered the airplane with a lever and wires. He was able to make the airplane go up and down.

Orville's flight was 10 feet (3 meters) above the ground and lasted just 12 seconds. He and his brother Wilbur made three more flights that morning. During the last flight, Wilbur flew the airplane a distance of 852 feet (264 meters) in 59 seconds. On December 17, 1903, the age of flight was born.

Wilbur Wright looks on as his brother successfully flies their airplane, *Flyer 1*.

The Wright brothers sent a message to their father which announced: "Success." How were the brothers able to succeed when others before them had failed? This is their story.

Orville's sketch shows how the toy helicopter his father had given him and Wilbur was put together. The brothers played with the toy they called the Bat until it broke. Then they built themselves a new one. Inset: a replica.

Chapter 1

How It All Began

Wilbur Wright was born in 1867. Orville was born four years later. They had two older brothers, Reuchlin and Lorin, and a younger sister, Katharine. The children constantly moved because their father, a minister, worked in many towns in the Midwest. In 1884, the Wright family finally settled in Dayton, Ohio.

When Wilbur and Orville were boys, their father bought them a toy helicopter. The helicopter was powered by a twisted rubber band. The boys were amazed that it could fly through the air.

Orville (left), age 9, liked to play jokes on family and friends while Wilbur, age 13, was more serious and intellectual.

Their parents had always encouraged them to be curious about how things worked. The boys made copies of the toy helicopter. They figured out how to make them fly. Playing with toy helicopters sparked Wilbur and Orville's interest in flight.

In 1892, Wilbur and Orville became interested in bicycles. They soon began to repair them for their friends. They opened a bicycle shop where they designed and built their own bicycles.

Three years after it opened, the Wright Cycle Company was a successful business, known for the custom-made bikes it produced.

The Wright brothers studied the gliders designed by German engineer Otto Lilienthal.

In 1896, Wilbur read about Otto Lilienthal, a German engineer who was interested in making a flying machine. He had already made 2,000 flights in gliders in Germany. The brothers began to read everything they could find about the science of flying.

One of the many glider designs by Lilienthal

Chapter 2

Controlled Flight

By the 1890s, many people had tried to build flying machines. All of these people faced several problems. How could they get the machine off the ground? How could they move it through the air? How could they control the machine during flight?

The Wright brothers decided that control was the biggest problem. They realized a machine would crash if it couldn't be kept steady in the air. To fly smoothly, the pilot would have to keep the wings of the flying machine balanced.

◀ Early flying machines were unable to get off the ground.

Wilbur had noticed that large birds like seagulls twisted the tips of their wings when they flew. This kept the birds from being blown about by the wind. The brothers built a kite with two sets of wings. Any flying machine with two sets of wings is called a biplane. The tips of the wings on the biplane kite could be twisted using wires. Wilbur was able to control the kite in flight by balancing its wings.

Wilbur and Orville learned how to control an aircraft in flight by watching large birds in flight.

The Wright brothers flew their gliders as kites before they piloted them.

Two men hold each side of the glider and run with it to help the pilot lift off into the air.

The next step was to build a biplane glider big enough to carry a pilot. While they were working on the glider, Wilbur wrote to the U.S. Weather Bureau. He wanted to find a place with strong winds where they could test their glider. Based on the information they received, the brothers decided on Kill Devil Hills on the Outer Banks of North Carolina.

In 1900, Wilbur and Orville traveled to Kill
Devil Hills to test their glider. First, they flew it
like a kite. Each brother controlled the wires
on one wing. Then, Wilbur piloted the glider.
He was able to control the glider as it flew! In
the next two years the brothers returned many
times to the Outer Banks. There, they tested
changes they had made to their gliders.

A Wind Tunnel

Wilbur and Orville needed to test which wing shapes flew best. To do this, they built a wind tunnel. The wind tunnel was a long wooden box with a fan at one end. The fan made a wind of about 30 miles (48 kilometers) per hour in the box. They tested different shaped wings in the wind tunnel. The wind tunnel was a great success. The brothers were able to test over 200 different styles of wings.

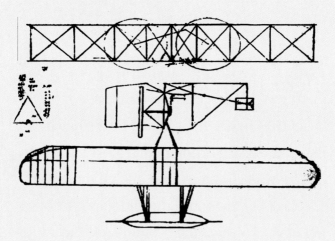

These diagrams show different views of one of the airplanes made by the Wright brothers.

This 1901 Wright wind tunnel was built with odds and ends the brothers found in their bicycle shop.

In October 1902, Wilbur Wright pilots
the third glider the brothers had built.

Wilbur and Orville discovered a problem with their gliders. They found they could only fly in a straight line. As soon as they tried to turn the glider left or right, they lost control.

They needed to find a way to turn. Again, nature and the birds they watched in flight gave them the answer. Wilbur and Orville learned that they needed to add a moveable rudder, or tail, at the back of the airplane. This would help the pilot control the glider up, down, and around.

In August 1902, Wilbur and Orville returned to Kill Devil Hills to test their third glider. They took turns flying. They made about 1,000 flights in the new glider. Soaring in the skies over the sand dunes, the Wright brothers learned to fly!

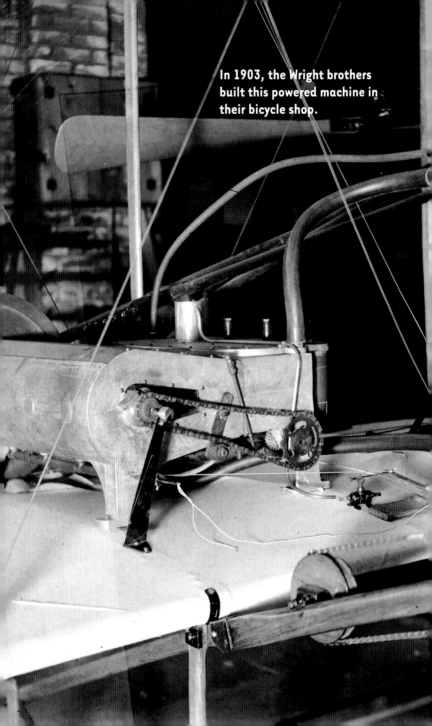

In 1903, the Wright brothers built this powered machine in their bicycle shop.

Chapter 3

Powered Flight

In October 1902, the Wright brothers left North Carolina. Back home, in Dayton, they were ready to build a powered flying machine. They thought about using an automobile engine, but these engines were too heavy.

Their bicycle mechanic, Charlie Taylor, helped them build a lightweight engine. They worked six weeks to build the engine. It took them another three months to design and build propellers. The propellers had wooden blades that spun around and made the airplane move forward.

Because it had an engine and propellers, the 1903 *Flyer 1* was heavier than any aircraft the Wright brothers had ever built.

The Wright brothers called their first powered plane *Flyer 1*. In September 1903, they went back to North Carolina to test their plane. After weeks of testing and adjusting, they were ready to fly. On December 17, 1903, Orville lay down in *Flyer 1* and took the controls. The flight lasted 12 seconds, but it was still a success. Orville Wright had made the first manned, powered airplane flight.

During its last flight, the rudder frame of the 1903 *Flyer 1* broke upon landing.

The brothers made three more flights that day. After the last flight, a strong wind smashed *Flyer 1* into the ground. The plane was badly damaged. The airplane was never flown again.

Flying *Flyer 1*

1. An elevator guided the airplane up or down. The pilot used a lever to move the elevator.

2. The wing wires allowed the pilot to balance the wings.

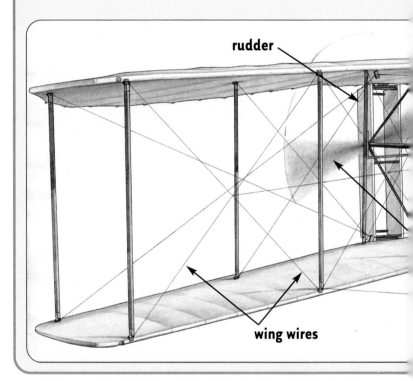

rudder

wing wires

3. The rudder, or tail, at the back of the airplane helped to turn the airplane. The pilot moved his hips to control the wing wires and rudder.

4. The propellers made the airplane go forward.

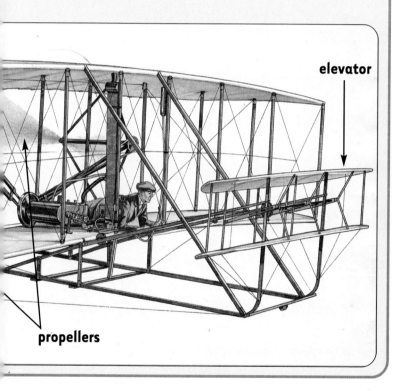

elevator

propellers

In 1909, Orville Wright and Lieutenant Lahm of the U.S. Army (Signal Corps) set a world record flying at about 40 miles (64 kilometers) an hour.

Chapter 4

The Business of Flying

After their historic flights, the Wright brothers returned home to Dayton. They wanted to do more work on their powered flying machine and to build a plane that they could sell. So, over the next few years, they experimented and tested aircraft in a farmer's field near their home. By October 1905, they had a practical airplane they could sell.

In 1908, the Wright brothers got contracts to build planes for the United States Army and the French government. The next year, they created the Wright Company to make and sell their planes.

European newspapers called Katharine Wright, pictured with her brothers in 1909, the "third Wright brother."

Their sister, Katharine, was a big help. She and her brothers were very close, and she had always encouraged them in their experiments. But Orville and Wilbur were not interested in the business of flying. They were interested only in the science of flying. So, Katharine took over the day-to-day operations of the new company and managed the business. She also traveled with her brothers to Europe to promote the *Flyer* and show how it worked. In 1910, she made her first flight with Wilbur in France.

Returning to the United States, Katharine and her brothers met President William Howard Taft. There was also a two-day celebration in her honor in Dayton. Newspapers at that time reported that there may not have been a "Kitty Hawk without Kitty Wright."

In 1912, Wilbur Wright died of a fever. He was only 45 years old. Three years later, Orville left the company the brothers had founded. He set up a small workshop where he would continue his work until his death in 1948.

The funeral of Wilbur Wright drew large crowds outside the church in Dayton, Ohio.

How to Write an A+ Report

1. Choose a topic.

- Find something that interests you.

- Make sure it is not too big or too small.

2. Find sources.

- Ask your librarian for help.

- Use many different sources: books, magazine articles, and Web sites.

3. Gather information.

- Take notes. Write down the big ideas and interesting details.

- Use your own words.

4. Organize information.

- Sort your notes into groups that make sense.

- Make an outline. Put your groups of notes in the order you want to write your report.

5. Write your report.

- Write an introduction that tells what the report is about.

- Use your outline and notes as you write to make sure you say everything you want to say in the order you want to say it.

- Write an ending that tells about your report.

- Write a title.

6. Revise and edit your report.

- Read your report to make sure it makes sense.

- Read it again to check spelling, punctuation, and grammar.

7. Hand in your report!

Glossary

biplane	any flying machine that has two wings
engineer	a person who uses science to design machines, roads, bridges, and other structures
glider	an airplane that uses wind rather than an engine to fly
lever	a control stick or bar that is used to move or raise something
power	to supply with energy
propeller	strong fanlike blades that spin and make an airplane go forward
rudder	the part of an airplane that helps the pilot turn the airplane

Further Reading

• Books •

Carson, Mary Kay. The *Wright Brothers for Kids: How They Invented the Airplane with 21 Activities Exploring the Science and History of Flight.* Chicago: Chicago Review Press, 2003. Grades 4–8, 160 pages.

Collins, Mary. *Airborne: A Photobiography of Wilbur and Orville Wright.* Washington, D.C.: National Geographic Society, 2003. Grades 5 and up, 64 pages.

Hunter, Ryan Ann. *Into the Air: An Illustrated Time Line of Flight.* Washington, D.C.: National Geographic Society, 2003. Grades K–3, 48 pages.

Old, Wendie. *To Fly: The Story of the Wright Brothers.* New York: Clarion Books, 2002. Grades 3–5, 48 pages.

Yolen, Jane. *My Brothers' Flying Machine: Wilbur, Orville, and Me.* Boston: Little, Brown Young Readers, 2003. Grades 2–4, 32 pages.

• Web Sites •

Library of Congress
http://memory.loc.gov/ammem/wrighthome.html/

National Air and Space Museum
www.nasm.si.edu/wrightbrothers

National Aeronautics and Space Administration (NASA)
http://wright.nasa.gov/orville.htm

National Park Service
www.nps.gov/archive/wrbr

Wright Brothers Aeroplane Company
www.first-to-fly.com

Index